Wisdom Teachings

Wisdom Teachings

PAULINE H. FIRKS

Copyright © Pauline Firks, 2004

First published in 1998 by Paper Doll
Second edition published in 2004
on behalf of the author

British Library Cataloguing-in-Publication data
A catalogue record for this book is available from the
British Library

ISBN 0-9547910-02

Printed by Cromwell Press, Trowbridge, Wilts

Contents

*All the teachings in this book
have been channelled through me
from my Spirit Guide,
Moo-Chow-Ching, without whom
this work would not have been
possible.*

Peace   Happiness   Eternity

I dedicate this book to the whole of the animal kingdom. I believe that while mankind continues to persecute and eat the animals there will always be pain and suffering on the earth plain.

WISDOM

When we grow up – we don't play at war.

Thought is often stronger than the written word.

If we are what we think we are we wouldn't have to prove it.

The more we know – the less we understand.

Occasionally out of the discordant comes harmony.

I

The nearer we get to the truth – the less we need to pretend.

We have to be taught until we learn.

What we want may not always be right for us.

Saints are the ones who walk amongst the sinners.

The people who stand back often see the most.

Our willpower is only as strong as the person who breaks it.

We have to balance the books of life.

Often where there is financial gain there is Spiritual loss.

Answers often come when you are not looking for them.

It's not how you look, but what you are that matters.

Walk away, and those who want to be
with you will follow.

It is only when we look back that we
can see what we have achieved.

There will be time enough for what we
are meant to do.

All life is a preparation.

Even a day can be a long time if it is
used wisely.

What is not to be lost will be found.

Life is full of lessons for us to learn.

Sometimes you must offend others in
order not to offend yourself.

Those who say the least may feel the
most.

Today is tomorrow – tomorrow is today.

There are no full stops in eternity.

It is not beauty of face, but beauty of heart that matters.

Eventually, all questions will be answered.

We will each receive what we have earned.

By teaching we learn ourselves.

To enjoy freedom we need some restriction.

It is up to those who are wiser to help those who are not.

Life _is_ the manifestation of the Spirit.

The wind is like a restless soul.

The ego is part of our lower self.

The more we act the less we live.

4

It is just as important to know when to stop as when to start.

When we feel we are superior true friends cannot be made.

The plans we have made may not be what has been planned for us.

The secret of life is to have just enough.

We will keep coming back until we get it right.

Life is education for the Spirit.

Death is of the body and not of the Spirit.

The wiser we are the less we have to say.

Until we think of other races as ourselves, disharmony will prevail.

Who will care for us if we don't care for them?

5

You can be knowledgeable and still be a fool.

Life is a brief interlude before eternity.

What you miss in one existence you learn from another – life is continual learning.

Them are us.

There must be some clouds in everyone's sky.

Everything has a beginning.

The miracle of life is the greatest miracle of all.

Life is the incarnation of the Spirit.

Grief goes deeper than tears.

There is a very thin line between being frightened and being brave.

Often the people with the best things to say are not heard.

We are born small to grow up.

If you have too much time just for yourself then you are not living correctly.

We are our thoughts.

If you are lost there is always a chance of being found.

Our body is just to borrow, but our Soul is forever.

Life is a place we visit.

At sometime we will all see the light.

The more you are the less you need to pretend.

We are all one.

We are all put to the test.

There is a record of everything.

What we don't experience this time, we must experience the next.

We will know all things in time.

Thoughts are living things.

What's ours is theirs.

If the foundation is shaky, you cannot build a strong house.

Life continually renews itself.

Eventually we will all believe.

Nothing can ever really be destroyed.

Where there is life – live it.

We have to keep searching until we find our true home.

Heaven and hell can be what we make it.

Tears cleanse the Soul.

Each rose has to bloom.

The devil can only get in where there is space for him.

The knowledge we have learnt cannot be taken away.

You can only take with you what you are.

Blessed are those who are content with what they have.

Eventually enemies will become friends.

Knowledge takes time.

Flowers will grow in any soil.

Age is immaterial to happiness.

When the question mark is removed it becomes positive.

The way of Truth is not easy.

Your heart can soar even if your body can't.

We should make provisions for the next world, not this.

The body is purely a medium for experience.

It is better to be a kind fool, than a hard wise man.

True life is in Spirit.

We are all on loan.

Life is a journey at which we never arrive.

Even the teachers have to be taught.

All has to be paid for – nothing is free.

We must always return home.

It is the spirit of Christmas that matters, not the surroundings.

Some of us are not big enough to understand.

Eventually we are found out for what we are.

Each Soul has to dawn.

We have to have known the bitter to appreciate the sweet.

We have to experience a thing ourself to know how the other person feels.

When we have to wait for something, it is all the sweeter when it arrives.

We don't have to experience something personally to know if it is right or wrong.

The more we get the less we can enjoy.

In order to know the end we have to go through the beginning.

Nothing is ours to own.

The end is just the beginning.

HUMOUR

A sense of humour is a sense of life.

Growing up and getting older aren't necessarily the same thing!

We don't necessarily have to be old to be wise!

Conversation usually flows when we talk about ourselves!

Usually people who get on with things don't talk about it!

Pretending takes a lot of effort!

Often when you have forgotten what you wanted it comes along!

Often we are told what we would like to hear!

If you know what to do – you should do it!

In pointing out others' faults – don't forget your own!

Those who think they don't have faults often have the most!

When we get what we are looking for it may not be what we want!

We may not always be right – even if we think we are!

We can all be good if we haven't had the opportunity to be bad!

Sometimes the story is more enjoyable than the event!

Some people think they can, but they can't, and some think they can't, but they can!

Don't write down what you have to do, just get on with it!

When something's available we don't always want it!

Things suddenly become very important when they happen to us!

Underestimate and be surprised!

We are only old when we think we are!

Being good requires working at!

Money only becomes important when you haven't got any!

Life is a mystery to those who don't understand it!

At the end of a bad day – remember, it could have been worse!

It doesn't take long to grow, but a long time to grow up!

No-one said it was going to be easy!

Nothing makes us as understanding as our own mistakes!

Often what we think is isn't, and what we think isn't is!

Lack of temptation can be lack of opportunity!

Leaving is sometimes better than arriving!

Some of us say it and don't mean it, and others mean it and don't say it!

Nothing is done until you do it!

We can always find energy for things we like to do!

It is only interesting while you are getting there!

There are more actresses off the stage than on!

Drink makes us sillier than we already are!

Too much talking wastes energy!

Adults are just bigger children!

Laughing clears headaches – frowning brings on headaches!

Some of the things we didn't receive we never needed anyway!

If we always waited until everything was right – we would never do anything!

If you want to keep looking back – the present can't be that good!

Some of us are big in size and small in stature!

It is always the unobtainable that seems so attractive!

To achieve perfection you have to keep working at it!

A smile always improves anyone's face.

REALITY

Often the reality is different from the dream.

Sometimes the memory is better than the event.

To be content is to give up.

Nothing goes by unnoticed – whether it be good or bad.

We are what we have experienced.

The best times are usually impromptu.

We see more of our true selves in a crisis.

We don't always know the best times until they have gone.

We are alive as much as our next heartbeat.

Only eternity is forever.

Often the only thing that holds us back is ourselves.

We can hide from other people, but not from ourselves.

Once we become used to change it is no longer change.

Our opinions are based on our experiences.

People become friendlier in common circumstances.

When things become scarce we take more care of them.

After the effort comes the reward.

It is only by doing something that we realise our capabilities and our limitations.

We often cause our own sickness.

We have to answer to ourselves.

The more we do something that is wrong, the more it seems right.

All the theory doesn't help the practice.

We only take chances with life when we don't know the importance of it.

Words are easy — it's the action that's hard.

The more you do the more you have time for.

The brighter moments are made even brighter by the dull.

Living _is_ today.

What we never try for we never gain.

When we lose one thing there is usually something else to take its place.

When you are happy you don't want to fight.

Whatever we think – it doesn't alter the truth.

Today's events are tomorrow's memories.

Sometimes the more time you have the less you achieve.

The more you have the more you have to give up.

We tend to treat the next person as we left the last.

It's only a fool that makes the same mistakes again.

It isn't what other people think of us, but what we think of ourselves that matters.

The less you have the more you look after it.

Sometimes we judge ourselves harder than we are judged.

Trust has no rival.

Confusion is all part of clarification.

Absence is a form of good-bye.

Things that take a while to build up usually last.

We are remembered for what we are.

The foundation bricks must be the strongest.

It is when we are at our worst that we are in most need of salvation.

Often your worst fears are never realised.

We will only listen if we want to hear.

Often things you are wishing for come when you least expect them.

All our thoughts are recorded.

Even a little seems a lot when you haven't got much.

If you are always searching for the next thing, you don't always enjoy what you already have.

There is often frustration before the realisation of a dream.

Our efforts seem all the more courageous when we don't know the outcome.

If all things came easily we wouldn't appreciate them.

We will stay the same if we don't want to change.

It is people who set the standards.

The ego can soon be deflated.

Mistakes are all part of living.

Without the pain we cannot have the pleasure.

Our childhood prepares us for life.

Energy is in the mind.

Because things don't appear to be changing on the surface, that doesn't mean they are not changing underneath.

We often trap ourselves.

Some of us are more guilty than the guilty.

Life is a series of changes.

The highlights of life are what we will
remember.

Our thoughts often weigh us down more
than our responsibilities.

Dates are not important – only the
events.

We rarely get lost when we know the way.

Often the worst has to come before the
best.

Pain is a way of paying back our debts.

Of all miracles, birth is the greatest.

Purity is a state of mind.

If we have too much choice, we often
can't decide on anything.

Without rules there is no order.

If we have too much freedom we can
often get lost.

How we see ourselves could be very different to how we are seen.

Even when we have the opportunity we don't always take it.

Time limits always get the job done.

Time is a gift.

Whenever you think you can't go on – you can often go further.

To make progress – a higher price must be paid.

Often we have to lose something to gain something else.

We often have to become a sinner before we become a Saint.

Even if we think we have everything, it is in fact only ours to borrow.

There is a Saint in the worst of us.

It is often the people who do the least that expect the most.

When we give up trying – we give up living.

Nothing comes from nothing.

Even freedom has restrictions.

Whatever you have suffered, someone has suffered before.

We often do more with less.

Circumstances dictate the outcome.

Anything that is worthwhile is rarely easy.

We don't always have to see something to know it's there.

We often blame others to alleviate our own conscience.

We take with us what we have learnt.

We can only speak to those who will understand.

We all need light to grow.

Optimism is a virtue.

Your brother is my brother.

Through change we grow.

Happiness is often found somewhere other than where we are seeking it.

It is usually people with the least who give the most.

The uncertainty of not knowing often keeps us going.

If we are happy it isn't always necessary to laugh.

We live up to the expectations that others have of us.

In the face of adversity we often perform our best.

Things often appear different from a distance than they are when we get close up.

Everything is there – we only have to look for it.

True determination continues in the face of opposition.

Beautiful things can still be found in ugly places.

People become closer when they have a common cause.

Events happen to teach us.

When we are too emotional we can't see clearly.

When you are helping someone else, your own worries disappear.

We have more understanding of other people's misfortunes when the same thing happens to us.

Things are forever moving – nothing stands still.

The time is <u>now</u>.

Our parents are our heritage.

Sometimes we go on our way too frightened to stop.

Change has to be prepared.

Some mistakes can take a lifetime to rectify.

Our mind can be free even if our body is trapped.

We can be strong in spirit, if not in body.

When you meet a kindred spirit the world seems in tune.

Majority often starts off as a minority.

Because the majority agrees it doesn't make it right.

You can often enjoy yourself more with the leftovers.

Time heals all things.

Time often distorts the truth.

The older you get the more important time becomes.

Interest brings energy.

When your character builds up – you don't need so many props.

Often it is necessary to become lost to find yourself again.

Make the best of your todays, they will be your yesterdays.

When you become involved – it's hard to be objective.

Simplicity needs no improvement.

Things happen to shake us out of our complacency.

A place is only as nice as the people in it.

It is easy to be nice when things are going well – it is when they are not that our true character comes through.

Simple things are the most poignant.

If we put ourselves on a pedestal we can easily fall off.

Things become more important when there is less time.

We need someone better to teach us.

It's the little touches that make things nice.

Even the different becomes the usual after a period of time.

What we have to wait for – we usually appreciate.

If we live each day as our last, we would achieve more.

Illness needs no appointment.

Total absorption means total living.

Imaginary barriers can be more insurmountable than real ones.

We often are what we think we are not.

Without variation everything becomes dull.

The longer we stay in one place – the older we feel.

Security is just an illusion.

We will only be lead if we really want to go.

When you play dangerous games you can get hurt.

We know in our hearts what is right.

Man-made power is illusionary power.

The less you have the less you lose.

We can be amongst something and yet still not really be involved.

It is only when our life is in danger that we realise the importance of life.

Sometimes the image is greater than the person.

If we don't see the light we remain in the darkness.

The plans of today are the foundations of tomorrow.

When the choice is too big it often stops us enjoying what we have.

Good health gives us a false security.

Each of us have our own fears to conquer.

We can only evaluate when we have something to evaluate by.

Friends need to be cultivated.

What isn't ours today – may be ours tomorrow.

We grow through effort.

We each have our own little miracles.

To be swayed, you have to have a leaning in that direction.

Sometimes it is best not to have what you want.

If we don't keep the mind occupied the mind occupies us.

The trouble with make believe is that you start to believe it.

After all the shouting we are still left with the facts.

Miles are only as far as we make them.

The seeds we plant today will take a little time to grow.

Life _is_ the lesson.

Life has many lessons.

All things are possible if you think they are.

Anything that makes us think is beneficial.

When you think there is nothing left, there is often a little more.

According to the circumstances our priorities change.

When you know the rules the game is easy.

Guilt is a form of repentance.

Memories record the event.

Waiting is part of receiving.

Wherever there is bad – good isn't very far behind.

Change is always gradual.

Evil starts off in a small way.

Most arguments are based on misunderstandings.

Tomorrow's success is brought about by today's trying.

You have to be aware to be frightened.

We can get help if we really need it.

Whatever happens – happens for a purpose.

Often the thought is worse than the action.

Sometimes the more time we have the less we achieve.

If we expect less it appears we receive more.

For every act of destruction there is an act of building.

To be arrogant is to hide inadequacy.

It is our purpose in life that keeps us going.

What is, is what has happened.

We choose what we want to be and how we want to live.

Too much freedom is no freedom at all.

The more we are given to do the more we will rise to.

Those who think they are the least worthy are often the most.

We learn by living.

Even accidents are planned.

In looking for one thing you can often discover something else.

If it's gone it was meant to.

When you have healed the mind you have usually healed the body.

We will only see what we want to see.

A thing is only of use when it is being used.

Making your way is often more enjoyable than being there.

We can get caught in our own trap.

Experience cannot be taken from us.

Life is for us to borrow.

As soon as the new is accepted it becomes part of the established.

Because we choose to believe otherwise – it doesn't mean it isn't so.

We are each other.

Sometimes we stand in our own light.

Our thoughts are often deeper than our words.

Sincerity is a job promised, carried out.

Whatever we have been given we have had to earn.

Obstinacy blocks us.

Things will only be prevented if they are meant to be.

We alter our opinions according to what suits us.

Life is how we see it.

You have had to have known fear to be brave.

It is usually the person with the quietest voice who has the most to say.

In time the pattern of life will reveal itself.

Flowers help to heal us.

We are all someone's son or daughter.

Often what is instant isn't lasting.

First the thought and then the action.

We have to tread the path we were meant to.

You can't serve too many masters.

You cannot live on regrets.

There is no questioning the Truth.

Reality often outlives the dream.

The oppressors will be oppressed.

If we could have everything there wouldn't be any choice.

Nothing is ever really wasted.

None of us are as good as we think we are.

It is the simple things that are the most enjoyable.

Those who fall to the lowest can also rise to the highest.

What we feel is often more important than what we know.

It is the ordinary things that keep us sane.

A time of reflection is never wasted.

The saddest heart can often rejoice the most.

When we like someone it takes a lot to dissuade us.

The truth is often different from what we would like it to be.

It is only in times of stress that we discover our true self.

We can hurt each other without violence.

Flowers are for us all to enjoy.

All things must change in time.

There can be fighting all around, but still peace within you.

Colour brings life.

Everything is constantly growing and renewing.

We can only be healed if we are ready.

Through uncertainty we become more certain.

There is only so much of anything you can enjoy.

Good work is true enjoyment.

The sun shines even on dark days.

The truth *is* the truth.

Our path is free to choose.

The effort comes first and the reward later.

The exploiters will be exploited.

Saying something affirms it.

Sometimes passing through is better than staying.

Even the strongest of us can be weak at times.

Having something to look forward to keeps us going.

Nothing calms and fills the soul like classical music.

Music transforms the humblest of surroundings.

You have to listen to music with your heart.

Music should be felt – not understood.

Life is involvement.

The positive needs no affirming.

Sometimes the predator becomes the prey.

No-one is beyond help.

Passing through isn't the same as staying.

We always remember people who spend time with us.

Effort never goes unnoticed.

We make excuses for people we like.

We can only go forward – not backward.

The right path is always the hardest.

Circumstances dictate the event.

We can only enjoy things when we need them.

You are where you should be.

Sometimes you have to leave something in order to appreciate it.

In all growth there is unsettlement.

The world starts with us.

You can walk through evil and still not be tempted by it.

Nothing teaches us about something as well as when we have to do it ourselves.

Most learning is done out of school.

Each of us is a miracle.

Through our children we are born again.

Sometimes, we have to find out what we're not, to find out what we are.

Phobias cut us off from reality.

You don't have to look something to be it.

Strength against weakness is not strength, but strength against strength is.

It takes age to understand.

Organisation precedes progress.

Guilt is part of repentance.

You can only appreciate freedom once you have experienced restriction.

Anything we are not sure about we register as fear.

Part of searching is finding.

49

Part of giving is receiving.

When you are involved it's hard to be objective.

THE ANIMAL KINGDOM

Animals have to fight for their existence against other animals, but when they have to fight against man also, it's an impossibility.

If it is wrong to take a humans life – what about an animals?

If animals could speak, we wouldn't dare abuse them.

51

The hunters will be hunted.

Treat animals with the respect they deserve.

While we continue to persecute and eat the animals there will be no peace in the world.

Animals give beauty and dignity to the world.

How can you not smile when a bird sings?

We must live side-by-side with the animals.

Animals are here to teach us and to heal us – contact with animals is very healing.

If you couldn't take an animals life – <u>don't</u> eat meat.

The more spiritual you become, the less you will need to eat flesh.

Meat eating belongs in the middle ages.

The trappers will be trapped.

Every animal has the right to kindness, and not to be eaten by humans.

Animals keep us sane.

All animals have a right to peace.

How beautiful the world will be when animals are allowed to live with man and not be used for food or material gain.

GUIDANCE

We can be brave in front of others, but it is when we are brave on our own that it really matters.

Help today – tomorrow may be too late.

Action without thought is no action at all.

It is not how a thing turns out – it's what we aim for that matters.

You don't get anywhere by not bothering.

No matter what we say, our action or non action shows what we really mean.

Sometimes it is better to keep silent.

In changing our attitude we can often change our lives.

There is nothing worse than constantly thinking we're right.

Whatever we give returns to us.

Always fight for what you believe in.

The attitude we adopt paves the way to how we are treated.

If we don't help others – who will help us?

If we hurt anything we in turn will be hurt.

Time can be taken from us – so use it wisely.

Try to keep cheerful through the gloom –
because the sunshine usually follows.

Give the best to someone else.

It is better to be free of mind – than free
of body.

Give flowers to the living, not the dead.

We must put back what we take.

Stay true to what you believe in.

The secret of life is adaptability.

Good will isn't saying, but doing.

Whatever you don't need – give away.

Those who don't appreciate what they
have soon lose it.

Whatever we have helped will never be
forgotten.

By accepting what is we can make more progress.

Try to build on what you have until it's more.

We can only enjoy things if we share them.

Follow your heart – not the book.

If you are always looking for faults – you often overlook the virtues.

Anything more than what you need is too much.

Always model yourself on the best – not the worst.

Don't just look on – participate.

The way to get through all your jobs is to set yourself little tasks each day.

We must all do what we think is right.

We have to be aware of what is wrong
  to be able to put it right.

Get the big things sorted out and the
  little things will fall into place.

In destruction we destroy ourselves.

Sometimes all we need is a direction.

If things are done for us – our initiative
  is taken away.

Sometimes thought can be more
  damaging than action.

Sometimes we need time for reflection.

We must keep searching until we find
  our true home.

In thinking of others we forget about
  ourselves.

Beautiful things can be done in the
  humblest of surroundings.

Never condemn anyone unless you have faced the same situation and done better.

In order to make something work we must put our hearts into it.

Wanting too much is a sign of immaturity.

True sin is knowing that something is wrong and still doing it.

It is no use looking without seeing.

It is no use listening without hearing.

Live to the dignity befitting you.

Those who retain the frivolous – can't be trusted with the serious.

Getting started is to be half-way there.

Don't give advice you wouldn't take yourself.

Whatever you are given – never take it
for granted.

Nothing is as bad when you stand up
and face it.

By accepting what we are not we can
make progress.

The shortcut is always the longest when
we don't know the way.

It's the trying that really matters – not
the results.

It is just as important to know when to
remain silent as to know when to speak.

When we are judging something – it
depends on what we judge it by.

It is often necessary for us to go through
what we are not, to find out what we
are.

If you are scared of something – look beyond it.

When you have a bad day think of all the good ones.

It is sometimes necessary to stand on our own to build our character.

If we rely too much on something when it goes we often fall.

Sometimes we become so involved with ourselves that we don't see what is going on around us.

It is often necessary to be quiet to get the right answer.

Don't ask for too much without giving something in return.

Economy is having just enough and managing.

It is a fool that stays the same all his life.

We don't win by cheating.

There is nothing more debilitating than inactivity.

All things are open to us, but it is our conscience that dictates what we do.

Pretence is such a waste of time.

If we live by looks alone we become vain.

We need to retreat sometimes in order to face the world again.

Be the first to stretch out a hand.

If we become too proud we are unapproachable.

When our interests are at heart it's hard to be unbiased.

In assessing your life add up the good things as well as the bad.

Motivation must start with ourselves.

It is not how lovely the body, but how lovely the spirit.

When you do something, do it wholeheartedly, or else it wouldn't have mattered if you hadn't done it at all.

Aim high – even if you fall low.

Unless we face up to our fears we will always remain frightened.

Push yourself a little further when you don't have to – in order to have extra reserve when you need it.

Don't use clever words where simple words will suffice.

Do the best you can with what you have.

We have to be aware of our failings to correct them.

Dispense with clutter.

Let go of what is holding you back.

Keep working through the rain, so that when the sun shines you have made some progress.

Pride halts our progress.

Time spent creating is never wasted.

The more civilised we become the more war will die out.

In judging others – don't forget to judge yourself!

In trying to be what we are not – we often forget what we are.

Don't plan too far ahead, do what you can today.

Don't be afraid, it's usually only the fear we are frightened of.

Accept whatever happens to us – we are meant to go through it.

The more we close in the less we can expand.

Keep aiming for your dream – it could be realised.

Let your mind run free and your body will follow.

Wait for a while and then things often look brighter.

Sometimes things have to be broken down to be built up again.

Try to finish existing ventures before starting new ones.

To give up is easy – to go on is hard.

Always find some joy in each day.

66

It is no use standing near the edge –
either jump in or move away.

Indifference is a form of lethargy.

If a thing is too new you can't enjoy it.

You have to be at ease with someone
before you can truly laugh with them.

There will always be obstacles if we put
them in the way.

When we hide from experience we hide
from life.

When we know our faults we are
half-way to putting them right.

Who else can we blame if we can't
blame ourselves?

Gentleness always wins.

When you feel low – look upwards.

News is best left until it's concrete.

Next time is often too late.

It is always better to have more to do than less.

Whatever you do – try to see it through.

It's our actions that show people what we are really like and not our words.

We become stronger by standing up for our beliefs.

If you are always living for the future, you don't live today.

People make the home – not the possessions.

When you start acting a part, it takes over.

When we think we are least ready, we are often the most prepared.

Always listen to your inner voice.

If we run away from fear it tends to catch up with us.

When we deceive others we are deceiving ourselves.

Usually the mind needs correcting before the body.

Often we have to prove we can do one thing, before we are given another.

If you seek an answer long enough you will find one.

When you get started everything falls into place.

Never say what you think people want to hear – only what you think is right.

You don't play games with life when you realise its value.

It's up to the strongest to help the weakest.

69

The less you have to rise to the more you give in to.

Let something go and if it belongs to you it will return.

Optimism is a good start to healing ourselves.

The more you suppress something that needs to be, the stronger it becomes.

Never judge by what is on top, always look underneath.

Problems are here for us to solve.

A firm hand is the kindest hand.

Never allow other people to dictate to you.

Don't gather unnecessary things around you.

Acting it, isn't being it.

If we never stretch ourselves, we never expand.

You cannot heal if you are not humble.

It takes a big heart to admit when we are wrong.

If you open up your eyes you can see further.

When we face up to something that frightens us we become stronger.

In order to be forgiven – we have to forgive.

In punishing others – we punish ourselves.

Never make possessions more important than people.

True giving is where there is no gain.

It's not what we have, but what we are that matters.

71

When you stand too close – you cannot always see the good points.

While we are struggling we are growing.

While we chase material things, we cannot find true happiness.

Each day is a day to treasure.

To heal things we have to be in sympathy with them.

You have to sift through the bad to get to the good.

With positive thinking you can make a lot of things better.

Negative thoughts bring negative results.

Try to ride the waves and not fight them.

Sometimes, it is as bad to stand back as it is to do nothing.

It is our working towards things that gives us our maturity.

Learning leads to learning.

Learn something every day.

Be content with what each day brings.

Sometimes, we have to do things we don't want to do in order to grow.

Never let the past hold you back.

You cannot hold on to what has gone.

You have to open up in order to receive.

Words don't mean anything unless they are meant.

Dreams will always be dreams unless they are realised.

Whatever you do – never expect anything in return.

Honesty always brings its own rewards.

Through only true repentance can we be forgiven.

We must learn to laugh at ourselves sometimes.

It doesn't matter if you have done things wrong – only that you have done them.

Always try to correct yourself first.

We have to give back what we have taken away.

It is only ourselves that can overcome what is weak within us.

Make time for laughter.

We all have to serve our apprenticeship.

Whoever takes life must be prepared to have their own life taken.

We must not ignore what we know to be right.

Whatever we break we have to repair.

Without forgiveness we cannot make progress.

Enjoy what you have at the moment.

Trap nothing, or one day you yourself will be trapped.

Friends have to be proven.

We often have to be cut back in order to grow.

We have to persevere in order to strengthen.

Take pleasure in little things every day.

Forgiveness is something we have to learn.

The best time to give is when you don't have much.

Our desire for wanting things traps us.

Never promise what you cannot do.

Sometimes we are not meant to know.

Narrow mindedness is a form of inwardness.

There are many avenues to explore before we arrive at the right one.

A smile is a reassurance.

Without effort you never get any reward.

Don't take anything you aren't given.

Live for what you have – not for what you hope to have.

To give up is not to go on.

It is only when we forget about ourselves
that we truly live.

Through adversity we can make Spiritual
progress.

Too many compliments make us
conceited.

In cutting off others we cut ourselves off.

We don't grow up by running away
from things.

Do not seek the approval of others –
only of yourself.

Our time is the greatest gift we can give.

We cannot run from ourselves.

What we learn today – we can teach others tomorrow.

The best way of learning things is to make your own mistakes.

We must free what is restricted.

You can influence more by being gentle than by being aggressive.

Laughter on a dull day is even better than on a bright day.

You can make progress while you are standing still if you think correctly.

Don't expect too much of others – only of yourself.

The best way of converting is by example.

We are each others responsibility.

If we try to change things by violence it won't last.

You can destroy material things, but never the Spirit.

We should always be true to ourselves.

Words are strong weapons – so be careful how you use them.

Sometimes we have to stop and gather our strength before starting anew.

The more you have the less you can account for.

What is stolen has to be put back.

If we keep standing at the threshold we will never know.

The only time we make true Spiritual progress is when we put aside the ego.

Without being tested – how can we expand?

Always take time to smell the flowers.

A day is a lot of time, if you use it wisely.

It is knowing when to say "no" that shows maturity.

Knowledge is only useful if you pass it on.

Peace comes from within – not without.

When we clear our prejudices we can make greater progress.

Always remember to say "thank you".

Always keep your goal in sight – never give up.

Perseverance usually pays off.

It is better to have real worries, rather than imaginary ones.

Hate takes energy.

Never use others discomfort for your own comfort.

Education is fine – so long as it leads to true thinking.

Often, when we are frightened of making mistakes, we make all the more.

From observation we learn a lot.

Visit the people you want to, today.

The wrong word at the wrong time can be disastrous.

Don't make problems.

You can't improve on simplicity.

Life isn't long enough for pretending.

It's the person that accepts life for what it is, that makes the most progress.

Never be too busy for the important things.

Water is healing and cleansing.

Confidence is in the mind.

Don't waste time by living in the past.

Jealousy is a negative element.

We should all live as one.

We often have to be cut back in order to grow.

We cannot be happy in pursuit of money.

There is nothing worse than constantly thinking you are right.

It is better to be honest in all things.

Try to do things without seeking praise.

If we thought of everyone as ourselves – we would care for everything.

To be too tidy isn't to live right.

Smiling does the most for your face and
spirit.

Sometimes we have to be pushed to stop
us falling.

RELIGION

The more we acknowledge religion the less we want to sin.

God has to remind us when we forget.

When we think no-one sees – God always does.

Without God at the centre we have no security.

There is no easy way to Heaven.

Christianity is in action not just words.

The less religious we are the more we need God.

When we get lost in God, we are found.

Often in a crisis we find faith.

God may forgive us before we forgive ourselves.

We can have everything and yet nothing at all without God.

God always holds the upper hand.

God is the Master.

God is always in control – we are pawns in the game.

Through the long road of life keep your eyes towards Heaven.

No-one can take away your beliefs.

We can't play with God's laws.

If you are searching for God – look at a flower.

When we are near flowers we are near God.

Creativity comes from God.

The only sanctuary is in God.

God never deserts us – it is we who desert God.

Religion is preached in Church, but lived outside.

God only lets us think we are in control.

We have to live to God's law.

God loves us for what we are – not what we think we are.

You can be a Christian without going to Church.

Home is in the Father.

To love God's world is to love God.

God's gifts are eternal.

In the end all Souls' must surrender themselves to God.

After periods of doubt our faith is restored even stronger.

God _is_ our conscience.

You have to believe for miracles to happen.

God works through people.

God is always at the helm.

It is usually people with the strongest faith who have doubts about it.

We will know how strong our faith is when we are tested.

We are never alone with God.

Never forsake God.

We must live to God's plan.

Without God we have no base.

The power of prayer is very strong.

God blesses those who bless.

We must seek God's approval before others.

The sincerest prayers are always heard.

We must all find God sooner or later.

We each have to give an account of ourselves to God.

There are many pathways to God.

In loving people – we are loving God.

We have to accept what God has planned for us.

There is no escaping the eye of God.

Don't seek recognition from people – only from God.

God is the Teacher.

Through God we learn.

When you pray you have to become the prayer.

All prayers are heard, but some are not meant to be answered.

LOVE AND COMPASSION

If we don't love one another we will destroy ourselves.

All children are our children.

Have respect for <u>all</u> life.

You will always return to wherever you receive love.

Love is not hurting anyone or anything.

True love isn't selfish.

To give of yourself is the greatest gift of all.

Where there is love there is no need for clever words.

Comfort anything that needs help.

It's not what's on paper – it's what's in your heart that matters.

Bless everything that breathes.

Love stays – infatuation goes.

Nothing is achieved without love.

Love is the highlight of life.

Compassion is part of our higher self.

The worse we are the more love we need.

To like the person when you know their faults is true friendship.

Love is shown by actions, not words.

Only by opening up our hearts can we truly grow.

Give love even if it isn't returned.

Do according to your heart.

Send out love and love returns.

The longer the parting, the greater the reunion.

Love knows no boundaries.

Sometimes a sympathetic word is all that is needed.

Be kind always.

Before hurting anything – imagine it was yourself.

Love breaks all barriers.

Say "I love you" before it's too late.

Love should be from day to day – not on occasions.

In helping others we help ourselves.

Marriage is in the heart.

We are all responsible for each other.

If we were to love everything we would all be in harmony.

Hate restricts us – love helps us to grow.

It takes a generous heart to give a true compliment.

True love accepts us for what we are.

In forgiving others we heal ourselves.

Love is the one who stands by you.

We have to have compassion for all things and forgiveness in order to make progress.

All life has a right to existence.

When all hearts have the same aim,
  things are soon achieved.

Romance is short lived, but love is forever.

True love is giving it to the other person.

Give things to people who need them the
  most.

Sometimes all that is needed is a word
  of encouragement.

A true gift is giving something that you
  would like to have.

If we let love lead the way we cannot go
  far wrong.

Love melts the hardest hearts.

Let everything you do be done with love.

Take care of <u>all</u> living things.

Without love – we only exist.

True kindness asks for nothing in return.

All loving thoughts are received.

Where there is love there is understanding.

True love doesn't need questioning.

Like a flower won't grow without water – people won't grow without love.

True love always stays.

Try to make all things happy around you.

We learn from people we love.

What is created in love cannot be destroyed.

Love teaches love.

If we are not kind to others – who will be kind to us?

You always go to the one who is kind to you.

You have to be loved to be missed.

The healers will be healed.

All the knowledge in the world doesn't matter if you don't have love.

Love is the greatest gift you can give.

We can only correct with love not hate.

Those with the greater love should give to those with the lesser love.

It is love that makes the home – not the furniture.

Compassion heals the Spirit.

Mans' saving grace is love.

All things are possible with love.

Healing is unconditional.

Treat all things as gently as you would like to be treated.

Be gentle with everything that isn't strong.

97

Romance is part of life.

All children need love to grow.

True love accepts us with our faults as well.

No kindness ever goes unnoticed.

Love teaches all.

In the end it is only love that matters.

Without love we die.